SEAHORSE CONNECTIONS

HELPING MY CHILD

A Guide to Supporting Reading

GRADE 1

SEAHORSE PUBLISHING

TABLE OF CONTENTS

THE SCIENCE OF READING

Reading is an essential skill for success in school and in life. In order to understand how children learn to read, parents should understand the science of reading.

The *science of reading* is a term that refers to more than 20 years of research by experts on how people learn to read. The research shows that reading does not come naturally. For many people, it takes significant effort. Learning how to read is most effective when it happens in a step-by-step process that is based on proven, research-supported strategies and techniques.

Good reading instruction has several important parts. It helps students develop skills in phonological awareness, phonics, fluency, vocabulary, and comprehension. All these skills help students build pathways in their brains that connect speech sounds to print and that connect words with their meanings. By using the science of reading as a guide, parents and teachers can support our children in learning how to read.

KEYS TO EFFECTIVE READING INSTRUCTION

Phonological Awareness: The ability to notice, think about, and work with the sounds that make up spoken words

Phonics: Understanding the relationship between sounds and the letters that represent them in written words

Fluency: The ability to read quickly and accurately

Vocabulary: Understanding word meanings

Comprehension: Gaining meaning from reading

CREATING SKILLED READERS

Reading is more than just sounding out words. Skilled readers are able to recognize words as well as understand their meanings on a deep level. They weave together memorization skills, phonics skills, vocabulary skills, background knowledge, and more.

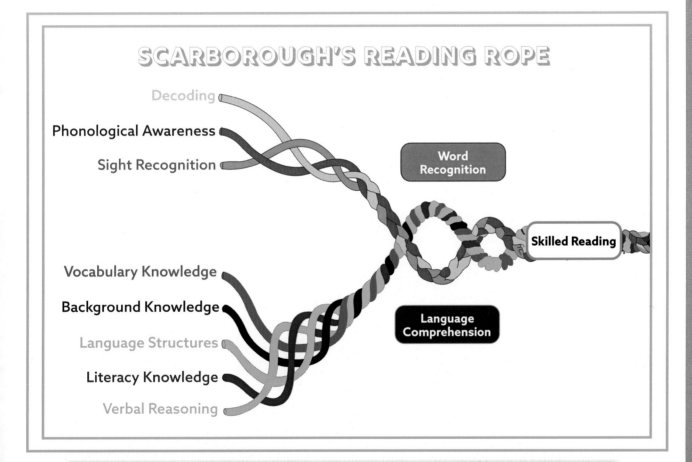

To show how children draw on a variety of abilities to become skilled readers, Dr. Hollis Scarborough created the Reading Rope. In 2001, this model was published in the *Handbook of Early Literacy Research* (Neuman/Dickinson).

PHONOLOGICAL AND PHONEMIC AWARENESS:
HEARING SOUNDS IN WORDS

Phonological awareness and phonemic awareness are important pre-reading skills. They describe a child's ability to hear, identify, and play with sounds in spoken language. These skills form an essential foundation for reading and writing development in first grade and beyond.

Children demonstrate phonological awareness when they recognize and manipulate, or change, parts of spoken words. Phonemic awareness is the last phonological awareness skill to develop. Children who have mastered phonemic awareness can hear, recognize, and play with the individual sounds, or phonemes, in spoken words.

PHONOLOGICAL AWARENESS MILESTONES

Ages 3 to 4	Produces real and pretend rhyming words
Ages 4 to 5	Claps or taps out syllables in words Recognizes words that begin with the same sound Segments or separates out each sound in words with three sounds Blends or combines individual sounds to produce words that have three sounds Counts the number of sounds in words that have three sounds
Ages 5 to 6	Segments or separates out each sound in words with four sounds Identifies the first and last sounds in a word Groups words with the same beginning sound Identifies which word does not rhyme in a set of three words Identifies which word is not the same in a set of three words
Ages 6 to 7	Deletes syllables from words when asked Deletes sounds from words when asked Substitutes syllables in words when asked Substitutes sounds in words when asked
Ages 7 to 8	Uses phonological awareness skills to spell words

ACTIVITIES FOR BUILDING PHONOLOGICAL AWARENESS

SYLLABLE HUNT

Look around the house to find things whose names have more than one syllable. Say the word and hold up a finger for each word part. For example, say, "bed-room" for bedroom and "ma-ca-ro-ni" for macaroni.

SWITCH IT

Think of a one-syllable word. Ask your child to change the beginning, middle, or ending sound in the word to make a new word. Use this example, reading letters shown in between slash marks as sounds.

Parent: Change the /st/ sound in *stop* to /sh/. What is the new word?

Child: Shop.

Parent: Great job! Now, change the /ō/ sound in *float* to /ă/. What is the new word?

Child: Flat.

Parent: Excellent thinking. Try changing the /nk/ sound in *sink* to /ng/. What is the new word?

Child: Sing.

Parent: Terrific! You did it!

WORD MAGIC GAME

The adult says a word. The child changes the beginning, middle, or ending sound to make a new word and says what changed. The adult changes the beginning, middle, or ending sound of the child's word to make a new word and says what changed. Keep going back and forth. How far can you go? Use this example, reading letters shown between slash marks as sounds.

Parent: Mop.

Child: Top. I changed /m/ to /t/.

Parent: Stop. I changed /t/ to /st/.

Child: Step. I changed /ŏ/ to /ĕ/.

Parent: Stem. I changed /p/ to /m/.

Child: Them. I changed /st/ to /th/.

Parent: Hmm. I can't think of a change that makes a real word. You win!

PHONICS:
LETTERS
MAKE
SOUNDS

Phonics is the knowledge that letters and combinations of letters represent sounds. This is an essential skill for beginning readers. Children who have the benefit of phonics instruction become better readers and spellers.

All words are made up of sounds. The word *dog* has three sounds. Each letter stands for one sound. The word *light* has three sounds. The letters *igh* represent one sound. The English language uses 44 sounds to make all words. However, there are only 26 letters in the alphabet. Some letters can make more than one sound. Other letters combine to make new sounds. This is like a code that beginning readers must figure out.

PHONICS BENEFITS
- Improved reading ability
- Faster ability to match sounds to letters
- Easier time sounding out unknown words
- Reading level increases faster

PHONICS 101
CONSONANT OR VOWEL?

Consonant letters are *b, c, d, f, g, h, j, k, l, m, n, p, q, r, s, t, v, w, x, y* (as in *you*), and *z*.

Vowel letters are *a, e, i, o, u,* and *y* (as in *my* and *baby*). Short vowels are marked with a curved symbol, like a smile on top: /ă/. Long vowels are marked with a horizontal line on top: /ā/.

ACTIVITIES FOR BUILDING PHONICS SKILLS

SHAVING CREAM LETTERS

Squirt shaving cream onto a large baking sheet. Spread it around evenly. Choose a letter or group of letters that makes a single sound. Say the sound. Use a finger to write the letter in the shaving cream and say its name. Say the sound the letter makes as you underline it. You can also do this with whipped cream!

SHORT VOWELS IN ACTION

Help your child remember short vowel sounds by associating an action with each one.

A: Pretend to bite an apple. Say, "I see a worm in my apple! Aaaah! Short *a* says /ă/ like what we said when we saw a worm in our apple!"

E: Slide your finger back and forth along the edge of a table. Say, "Eh-eh-edge. Short *e* says /ĕ/ like the beginning sound in *edge*."

I: Scratch your nose. Say, "I have an ih-ih-itch. Short *i* says /ĭ/ like the beginning sound in *itch*."

O: Open your mouth as if the doctor is checking your throat. Say, "Ahhhh. Short *o* says /ŏ/ like the sound you make at the doctor."

U: Point upward. Say, "Uh-uh-up. Short *u* says /ŭ/ like the beginning sound in *up*."

KEEP IT SHORT

To avoid confusing beginning readers, don't add a vowel sound when you make consonant sounds. For example, the sound for letter *t* is /t/, not /tuh/.

RAINBOW LETTERS

Draw a set of rainbow arches with space in between. Under the rainbow, write a letter or group of letters that makes one sound. Then, begin with the top arch. Use a red marker or crayon.

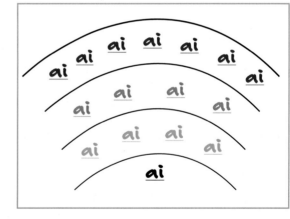

Follow these steps:

1. Say the sound the letter or letters make.

2. Write the letter or letters and say their names as you write.

3. Underline the letter or group of letters and say the sound it makes.

Repeat until the first arch is filled. Then, use an orange marker or crayon to fill the second arch in the same way as you say, write and spell, underline and read. Repeat for the next arches using different colors.

IS IT A REAL WORD?

Write a list of consonant letters. On a sticky note, write the stem of a word family, such as **-at, -en, -id, -ot,** or **-ug.** Put the sticky note next to each consonant. Does it make a real word?

9

DECODING:
SOUNDS MAKE WORDS

Decoding is the ability to sound out written words. Children use their knowledge of the phonics code to figure out words. A child with strong word decoding skills will have better reading comprehension skills.

When your child can see a word, understand the sound each letter represents, and blend sounds together to say the word, they are decoding. Once they can decode words independently, they have the tools they need to begin reading with fluency and comprehension.

SOUNDING OUT WORDS

Segmentation means breaking a word into its individual sounds.
dog: /d/ /ŏ/ /g/   **sheep:** /sh/ /ē/ /p/

Blending means putting the sounds in a word together without pauses. Try these techniques to help your child with blending.

Continuous Blending: Stretch out each sound so that it continues into the next. Use your finger to slide across each letter from left to right.
sip: sssssssssssssiiiiiiiiiip

Final Blending: Blend the first sounds together and then add the final sound.
sip: si-p

Isolated Blending: Say the first sound the loudest and then say each following sound softer. The last sound will be the softest.
sip: S i p

ACTIVITIES FOR BUILDING DECODING SKILLS

HIGHLIGHT IT
Use two different colors to highlight the consonant letters and vowel letters in a list of words.

bed   plan

MARK IT
In a list of words, mark vowel letters *v* and consonant letters *c*. Underline any letters that go together (vowel teams, consonant blends, consonant teams, etc.).

b e d   pl a n
c v c   cc v c

BOX IT
In a list of words, draw boxes around letters that go together.

b e d   pl a n

MAGIC E RAINBOW
Some words have the pattern vowel-consonant-e. The final *e* is called magic *e*, bossy *e*, or silent *e*. The vowel is long and says its name. Use this strategy for remembering the rule.
1. Write *v* under the vowel and *c* under the consonant that follows it.

game
v c

2. Cross out *e*. Draw an arch to connect *e* to the vowel. Say, "*E* makes the [vowel name] say [vowel name]." Example: "*E* makes the *a* say *a*."

game
v c

3. Sound out the word: /g/ /ā/ /m/.

SIGHT WORDS AND HIGH-FREQUENCY WORDS:
BUILDING BLOCKS FOR SUCCESS

Knowing sight words and high-frequency words helps create a strong foundation for beginning readers. Both types of words are often used in reading and writing. A sight word is a word that does not follow the regular rules of phonics and spelling. It is not decodable or is very difficult to decode. High-frequency words are decodable words that students need to know in order to be fluent readers. However, the phonics rules needed to decode them might not have been taught yet.

The word *like* is a high-frequency word. It can be decoded using the "magic *e*" or "bossy *e*" rule. Children who are just learning to read words such as *cat* and *sit* have not been taught this rule. However, since *like* is used in many simple stories, it is often introduced as a high-frequency word.

The word *have* is a sight word. It occurs often, but it does not follow the "magic *e*" or "bossy *e*" rule. Therefore, this word must be memorized, or identified by sight.

GETTING UNSTUCK

What to do when your child gets stuck reading a word, or when they decode a word incorrectly? Allow time for your child to figure it out. Gently offer these strategies.

- Spell the word.
- Ask, "Do you see any letters that go together?"
- Ask, "Do you see any little words inside the longer word?"
- Say, "Let's sound out each part."

SMALL BUT MIGHTY

Just 13 words make up 25 percent of all English words in print.

a
and
for
he
in
is
it

of
that
the
to
was
you

ACTIVITIES FOR LEARNING SIGHT WORDS AND HIGH-FREQUENCY WORDS

Slap It!

Choose five words to learn. Write each on a sticky note. Place the notes around the house. When your child finds a word, have them read the word and then use their hand to slap it.

COLORFUL WORDS

Write a word in the middle of a sheet of paper. Have your child choose a colored marker or pencil. Read the word. Have your child write the word in color, saying the name of each letter aloud as it is written. Underline the word from left to right while reading the word. Then, choose a new color and repeat. Keep choosing new colors until you have filled the page.

Trace It

Write words on index cards. Have your child read each word aloud. Ask your child to use their index finger to trace each letter while saying its name. Then, use a finger to underline the word from left to right while reading the word. Repeat with the next card.

FLUENCY: READING WITH EASE

Fluency is the ability to read with reasonable speed and expression. A fluent reader doesn't have to stop to decode each word. They can focus on what the story or text means. Fluency is the bridge between decoding words and comprehension.

Your first grader is on the road to learning how to read smoothly. When your child reads aloud, encourage them to change their tone and expression to match the meaning of the words and what is happening in the story. By the end of the school year, your child should be reading about 70 words per minute. The best way to reach this speed is to practice, practice, practice.

THE FIVE FINGER RULE

How do you know if a book is at the right level of difficulty for your child? Teach your child this trick.

ACTIVITIES FOR BUILDING FLUENCY

BOOK OF THE WEEK CHALLENGE

Choose a book that has about 20 to 30 words. It is okay if the words or sentences repeat. On Sunday, read the book together at least once. Set a timer and have your child read it aloud. Record the time it takes your child to read. Note if your child needed help. Read the same book on Monday. Time your child again and note if help was needed. Continue the process every day for a week. At the end, show your child the evidence of how they are improving in fluency.

ECHO READING

Choose a favorite book on your child's reading level. You read the first sentence as your child slides a finger along the words. Have your child echo the first sentence as you slide your finger along the words. Then, you read the next sentence as your child slides a finger. Your child will echo the second sentence as you slide your finger. Continue the process until you have read the whole book. Remember to change your voice to respond to what is happening in the story. Encourage your child to change their voice, too.

1. Begin reading the book. Hold up your fist.

2. Put up a finger each time you find a word you don't know.

3. If you put all five fingers up before you are done with the book, it is too challenging. Try another book until you find one that is just right for you.

VOCABULARY:
WORDS HAVE MEANING

Vocabulary plays a critical role in the process of learning to read. Young readers use their knowledge about words to make sense of what they are reading. In order to understand what is read, a child must know what the words mean. Children need a large mental "word bank" to draw on as they read. The larger a child's vocabulary, the more they are able to comprehend what they are reading or listening to.

As new words are encountered, children link them to words they already know to add to their growing vocabularies. Some words are learned naturally. Others must be taught. Children learn new words through daily conversations and by having experiences that teach them about the world. Reading books to your child also exposes them to rich language.

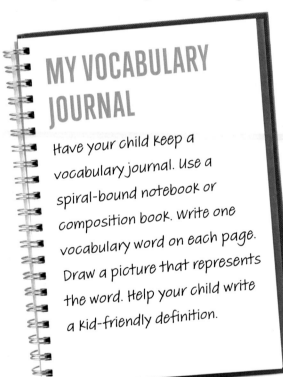

MY VOCABULARY JOURNAL

Have your child keep a vocabulary journal. Use a spiral-bound notebook or composition book. Write one vocabulary word on each page. Draw a picture that represents the word. Help your child write a kid-friendly definition.

feast

lots of food to eat

TYPES OF VOCABULARY

Listening Vocabulary: The words we hear
Speaking Vocabulary: The words we say
Reading Vocabulary: The words we read
Writing Vocabulary: The words we use to write

ACTIVITIES FOR BUILDING VOCABULARY

NEW WORD TALK

Introduce a new word to your child by providing a simple definition. Then, give an example that relates to your child's experiences. Have your child think of an example, too. Over the next few days, take the opportunity to use the new word in conversation.

WORDS FROM NONFICTION

Choose a nonfiction book. Read the book aloud to your child. Talk about new words from the book. Have your child share with others the new words they learned.

NEW WORDS WHILE READING

When your child is reading, it is okay to stop to discuss a new word. Reread the sentence and ask what your child thinks the new word means. Give a child-friendly definition. Help your child make a personal connection to the word.

COMPREHENSION:
UNDERSTANDING
WHAT IS READ

Reading comprehension is the essence of reading. It is the ability to gain meaning from what you read. This is a complex skill that develops over time. Children can begin growing in this area by taking time to think about what they have just read. As children read, their minds must be "turned on" and thinking actively about what they are reading.

First graders should be able to understand books they read and books that are read to them. They can show their understanding of fiction books by retelling the story and describing the characters, setting, and events. After reading a nonfiction book, they can tell important facts they learned.

ACTIVE READING

Active reading happens when the reader is involved and engaged with the text. The reader is thinking about what is being read and making connections. This type of reading is essential for comprehension.

You can help your child become an active reader by remembering A-B-C.

A: Ask questions about the reading.

B: Build vocabulary by learning new words from the reading.

C: Connect the reading to your child's own experiences.

ACTIVITIES FOR BUILDING READING COMPREHENSION

SHARED READING

Choose a book. Read aloud the first paragraph or first couple of sentences. Talk about what was read. Have your child read the next paragraph or couple of sentences. Continue to discuss the story as you share the reading.

MAKE A NOTE (NONFICTION BOOKS)

Fold a sheet of paper into fourths. In the center of the paper, write the main topic of the book. Then, in each section, write and illustrate a fact about the topic.

BEGINNING-MIDDLE-END (FICTION BOOKS)

Fold a sheet of paper into thirds. In the first section, draw and label a picture of what happened in the beginning of the story. In the second section, draw and label a picture of what happened in the middle. In the third section, draw and label a picture of what happened at the end of the story. Use the drawings to talk about and retell the story.

COMPREHENSION QUESTIONS

For Informational Texts (Nonfiction)

Key Ideas and Details

- How do you know ___? How is ___?

- What do you think the author wants readers to know?

Craft and Structure

- What does the word ___ mean? How do the other words help you figure it out?

- What categories would you put these in? What are examples of things that are ___?

- Why did the author put a heading on the sections? How does it help you?

Integration of Ideas and Knowledge

- What does this picture show? How does it help you understand the words?

- Why does the author say that ___ happens?

For Literary Texts (Fiction)

Key Ideas and Details

- Where does the story take place?

- Who are the characters? What do we know about them?

- What happens at the beginning, middle, and end of the story?

Craft and Structure

- What words in the story tell how the character feels?

- Is the story realistic or fantasy? How do you know?

Integration of Ideas and Knowledge

- How would a character from a different story act if they were in this story?

- How is this character like you? How are they different?

WRITING:
HANDWRITING

Knowing how to write letters by hand smoothly, quickly, and legibly is essential for school success. Even though much schoolwork today is done on a computer, students are often asked to write by hand for jotting notes, taking tests, and completing homework. Taking time in the early grades to develop handwriting skills can prevent academic difficulties in the future.

When first graders write letters at the same time they are learning letter sounds, both skills are reinforced, leading to improved reading, writing, and spelling. With practice, handwriting becomes automatic. Students don't have to think about the formation of each letter, and they are free to focus on the meaning of what they are writing.

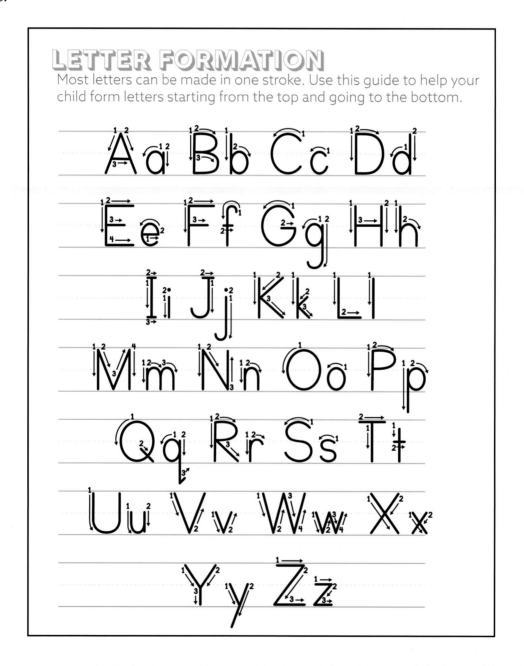

LETTER FORMATION
Most letters can be made in one stroke. Use this guide to help your child form letters starting from the top and going to the bottom.

ACTIVITIES FOR BUILDING WRITING SKILLS

PREVENT CONFUSION FOR b AND d

Because lowercase *b* and *d* look so similar, children often get them mixed up. To help your child, try these tricks.

To remember the letter *b*, associate it with a bat and a ball. Write a line from top to bottom for the bat. Then, trace the line up just a little and form the circle for the ball.

To remember the letter *d*, sing the first part of the ABC song: A-B-C-D. Then, write the letter *c*, starting at the top. When you complete *c*, continue the line upward to form *d*.

SHAPE SORT

Work with a set of magnetic letters on the fridge, a baking sheet, or another surface. Help your child sort the letters in different ways. Make a group of letters that have circles or curved lines, a group of letters that have straight lines, a group of letters that have tails, etc. As your child touches each letter, ask them to say its name and the sound it makes.

FIND IT, FIX IT

Provide a magnifying glass and show your child how to use it to look at letters they have written. Prompt your child by asking them to find an uppercase letter, a lowercase letter, a letter with curved lines, a letter that touches the top line, a letter that shows fabulous handwriting, a letter that might need fixing, etc.

WRITING:
SENTENCES

Your first grader is learning to put words together to write simple, complete sentences. This effort is made easier by practicing other reading and writing skills: handwriting, recognizing high-frequency words and sight words, using phonics skills to decode words, and learning vocabulary words. Building skills in all these areas supports young writers.

First graders show understanding that writing proceeds from left to right and continues on to the next line. They are beginning to start each sentence with a capital letter and end it with a period or other punctuation mark. First grade writers are learning that a sentence contains a subject part and a verb part.

HELP WITH SPACING

If your child is having a hard time leaving space in between words, show them how to use a spacing tool. It can be a Lego brick, a paper clip, or even their own index finger. Place the tool after each word to judge how much space to leave before the next word. Remind your child that letters within each word like to be very close together. They should almost touch.

ACTIVITIES FOR BUILDING WRITING SKILLS

TYPES OF SENTENCES

A statement ends with a period: Luna wakes up**.**

A question ends with a question mark: What is today**?**

An exclamation ends with an exclamation mark: It is her birthday**!**

LETTER, WORD, OR SENTENCE?

Make sure your child knows the difference between a letter, a word, and a sentence. Print out a simple story for your child and read it together. Then, provide a highlighter. Can your child highlight one letter? One word? One sentence?

DOES SPELLING COUNT?

What should your child do when they are writing a first draft and do not know how to spell a word? Encourage them to get their ideas down by using invented spelling, or writing any letters they think may be in the word. Then, they can circle the word. After the draft is complete, review the circled words. Help your child sound out the correct spellings or provide the correct spellings.

Sentence Building

On one set of index cards, write subjects that begin with capital letters. On another set of index cards, write verbs followed by a period. Can your child match the subjects and verbs to form sentences? Encourage them to write and illustrate the silly sentences they make.

Frogs   ride.
Kids   fall.
Trees   splash.
Robots   dance.
Cookies   yell.

WRITING: SHOWING
UNDERSTANDING

Children are often asked to write about what they read. They also write to tell about their own ideas. When children write, they show their understanding of phonics, high-frequency words, vocabulary, and more. They demonstrate that they have internalized what they have learned and made it their own.

First graders are learning how to use sentences to write stories, reports, and opinions about a variety of topics. By the end of the year, they can think about what to write, write sentences to show their ideas, review their work, and add details. When they write, first graders use a combination of invented spelling and correct spelling.

WHEN WRITING IS HARD

- Use a text-to-speech feature on a computer. Then, have your child copy on paper.
- Have your child tell you what to write. Help them create the sentences. When you are finished, your child can copy what you wrote.
- When your child starts writing, set a timer for five minutes. When the timer goes off, take a five-minute break. Continue this pattern until the writing is complete.

ACTIVITIES FOR BUILDING WRITING SKILLS

KINDS OF THINGS

Write a topic such as *favorite foods* or *animals with tails*. Ask your child to list three examples that fit the category. Then, help your child use the list to write a four-sentence paragraph. Use this example.

Bailey's Favorite Foods

pizza

strawberries

carrots

Bailey has many favorite foods. She likes pizza with cheese. She likes red strawberries that taste sweet. She likes carrots with butter and salt.

DETAILS, PLEASE

Choose a nonfiction book. Write the book's topic in the center of a sheet of paper and circle it. As you and your child read, write details inside more circles that surround the center circle. Draw a line to connect each detail circle to the topic circle. Once there are at least four details, help your child write a simple paragraph about the topic.

SPELLING:
USING THE CODE

When children sound out a word, they use their knowledge of the phonics code to decode it. By contrast, when they spell a word, they use their knowledge of the phonics code to encode it. They must match a letter or group of letters to each sound heard in a word. Children can usually read words before they can spell them. But practicing spelling improves reading ability. Good spellers are generally good readers, and vice versa.

First graders are learning to spell three-letter words with the CVC, or consonant-vowel-consonant, pattern. These are often grouped into families of words that end with the same vowel and consonant. For example, the *-ap* family includes *cap*, *tap*, and *lap*. By the end of the school year, first graders are learning to spell four-letter words with consonant blends (as in *frog* and *plan*) and long vowel sounds (as in *like* and *cake*).

LEARNING TO SPELL RULE-BREAKERS

Many English words do not follow phonics rules. But it is still important for children to know how to spell them. Try these strategies.

Say, Spell and Write, Read and Underline: Say the word. Write the word while saying the name of each letter. Underline the word from left to right as you read it. Repeat five times in a row.

Triangle Word: Say the word. Write the first letter. Say the word. Write the first two letters. Say the word. Write the first three letters. Continue the pattern until the word is written. Then, say the word and write the full word three more times. See the example at right.

d
do
doe
does
does
does
does

Trace It: Write the word and read it. Trace each letter with your finger as you say its name. Use your finger to swipe under the word from left to right as you read it. Repeat three times. Then, close your eyes and use your finger to write each letter of the word in the air.

ACTIVITIES FOR BUILDING SPELLING SKILLS

NOTICE PATTERNS
Have your child look at a group of words and note any patterns. For example, "I see /ag/ is spelled *a-g* at the end of the word." Study these words together.

ROLL IT

Write 20 letters, sight words, or three-letter words on index cards. If older children will play, make separate cards with words at their level. Players roll a die and draw that many cards. Read the words or say the letter sounds. If the player can say the letter or spell the word, they keep the card. The first player with 10 cards wins.

I SPY

Write eight to ten spelling words on a sheet of paper and show it to your child. Then, give clues to the words. When your child spies the word, they should say it and spell it. Use this example.

Parent: I spy a word that begins with *h* and means "jump."
Child: Hop. *Hop* is spelled *h-o-p*.

DO I USE C OR K?

When writing a word that begins with the /k/ sound, how do you know which letter to use? It depends on which vowel letter follows it. This rhyme will help: *C* goes with *a, o,* and *u,* and *k* goes with the other two (*e, i*). Try it with words such as *kid, can, cut,* and *keep.*

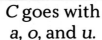

C goes with *a, o,* and *u.*

K goes with the other two.

WHAT TO DO
WHEN YOUR
CHILD STRUGGLES

As a parent, it is frustrating when your child has difficulties. When this happens, it is important to seek out help. Begin with your child's classroom teacher, who might be able to provide more personalized instruction and strategies to try at home. You can also reach out to a reading specialist or special education teacher at your school or district. Tutors, professionals in private practice, and reading clinics are other ways to support your child.

If your child continues to struggle, ask the school to have a meeting that includes the classroom teacher, reading or literacy coach, school psychologist, school counselor, and special education teacher. This is an opportunity for everyone to be honest and open in a supportive way. The goal of such a meeting is to gather information in order to decide how to move forward. Some possible outcomes are formal evaluation for special education, creation of a 504 Plan or Individualized Education Plan (IEP), more intensive instruction by the classroom teacher, or referral to a pediatrician for a possible medical diagnosis.

QUESTIONS FOR TEAM DISCUSSION

- Are there attention issues at school? At home?
- Is poor attendance having an impact?
- When were the child's hearing and vision last checked?
- Does the child speak another language?
- Did the child struggle with reading in previous grades?
- What supports and strategies have been in place? Were they successful?
- Does the child have a medical condition that may impact learning?

HOW TO HELP AT HOME

If your child is reading below grade level, you'll want to enlist the support of their classroom teacher and other experts. However, you have an important role to play. Your encouragement can make a big difference when it comes to your child's attitude about reading, motivation to read, and steady growth as a reader. Try these suggestions.

1. NOTICE STUMBLING BLOCKS

Not all reading problems are alike. You are in a unique position to notice when and why your child is struggling. Read with your child and take note of what is challenging. Then you'll be able to make a plan for getting help. Some reasons for concern are avoidance of reading, slow and labored oral reading, and having trouble with books well below grade level. Share specific observations and concerns with your child's teachers.

2. KEEP READING

Make reading every day a joyful part of your home. Make sure your child has easy access to a variety of reading materials. Let your child see you reading for pleasure and for finding information. Talk about what you are reading and encourage your child to talk about what they are reading. This will lead to rich conversations that help your child build vocabulary and language skills.

3. FIND THE RIGHT BOOKS

Let your child choose books that interest them. Seek out books that relate to your child's interests. Reading books in a series is a good way to encourage reading comprehension as children become familiar with different stories about the same characters. Graphic novels and early chapter books can help children bridge from picture books and read-alouds into more independent reading.

4. HAVE FUN

Sometimes, children get the message that reading is a chore. Make it fun by encouraging your child to draw pictures and write stories about favorite characters, act out stories, and take turns reading aloud with you or with a sibling. By joining in the fun, your child will steadily build skills and grow as a reader.

WORDS TO KNOW

504 Plan: a plan that describes the accommodations that the school will provide to support the student's education

active reading: when a reader is thinking about, involved with, and engaged in a text

decoding: the ability to sound out written words

ELA: English language arts

ELL: English language learner

ESE: exceptional student education

fluency: the ability to read with speed, accuracy, and appropriate expression

high-frequency word: a word that often appears in written material and that can be decoded using common phonics rules

IEP: individualized education plan; a personalized plan that describes the special education instruction, supports, and services a child needs

Lexile level: a scientific measurement of the complexity and readability of a text

literacy: the ability to read and write

phonemic awareness: the ability to identify and manipulate individual sounds in spoken words

phonics: matching the sounds of spoken English to individual letters or groups of letters; the relationship between sounds and letters

phonological awareness: the ability to identify and manipulate syllables and other parts of spoken words

reading comprehension: the ability to understand and interpret what you read

RTI: response to intervention; an educational strategy that aims to identify struggling students early on and give them the support they need to succeed in school

science of reading: a body of research that shows what is most important and effective in reading instruction

sight word: a word that often appears in written material and that can be difficult to decode using common phonics rules

standards: simple statements that describe what students are expected to know or do as a result of what is learned in school

syllable: a word part that contains one vowel sound

Tier 1 instruction: instruction for the whole class that is based on the learning standards for that grade level

Tier 2 instruction: small group instruction for students who demonstrate slight learning challenges in specific areas

Tier 3 instruction: small group instruction for students who need more intensive help and support

vocabulary: knowledge about what words mean

ADDITIONAL INFORMATION

To learn more about the science of reading:
https://teacherblog.evan-moor.com/2022/05/02/what-parents-need-to-know-about-the-science-of-reading/

To learn more about phonological awareness and phonemic awareness:
https://readingteacher.com/what-is-phonological-awareness-and-why-is-it-important/

To learn more about phonics and decoding:
https://www.twinkl.com/teaching-wiki/decoding

To learn more about vocabulary development:
https://www.edutopia.org/article/6-quick-strategies-build-vocabulary/

To learn more about reading comprehension:
https://www.readnaturally.com/research/5-components-of-reading/comprehension

To learn more about IEPs and 504 Plans:
https://www.understood.org/en/articles/the-difference-between-ieps-and-504-plans

Some information for this book came from the following websites:
- Florida Center for Reading Research https://fcrr.org
- Home Reading Helper https://www.homereadinghelper.org
- International Dyslexia Association https://dyslexiaida.org
- North Carolina Department of Public Instruction https://www.dpi.nc.gov
- Reading Rockets https://www.readingrockets.org

Written by: Madison Parker, M.Ed.
Design by: Rhea Magaro-Wallace
Series Development: James Earley
Editor: Kim Thompson

Photo credits: Shutterstock

Library of Congress PCN Data
Helping My Child with Reading First Grade / Madison Parker, M.Ed.
A Guide to Supporting Reading
ISBN 979-8-8904-2112-8 (paperback)
ISBN 979-8-8904-2122-7 (eBook)
ISBN 979-8-8904-2132-6 (ePUB)

Printed in the United States of America.

Seahorse Publishing Company

www.seahorsepub.com

Published in the United States
Seahorse Publishing
PO Box 771325
Coral Springs, FL 33077